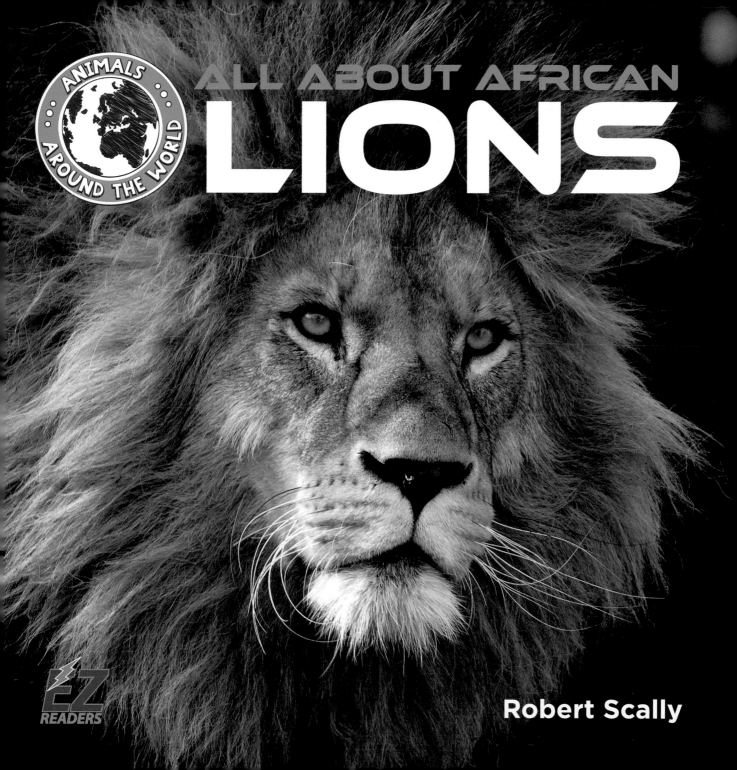

ALL ABOUT AFRICAN
LIONS

ANIMALS AROUND THE WORLD

EZ READERS

Robert Scally

Creating Young Nonfiction Readers

EZ Readers lets children delve into nonfiction at beginning reading levels. Young readers are introduced to new concepts, facts, ideas, and vocabulary.

Tips for Reading Nonfiction with Beginning Readers

Talk about Nonfiction
Begin by explaining that nonfiction books give us information that is true. The book will be organized around a specific topic or idea, and we may learn new facts through reading.

Look at the Parts
Most nonfiction books have helpful features. Our *EZ Readers* include a Contents page, an index, and color photographs. Share the purpose of these features with your reader.

Contents
Located at the front of a book, the Contents displays a list of the big ideas within the book and where to find them.

Index
An index is an alphabetical list of topics and the page numbers where they are found.

Glossary
Located at the back of the book, a glossary contains key words/phrases that are related to the topic.

Photos/Charts
A lot of information can be found by "reading" the charts and photos found within nonfiction text. Help your reader learn more about the different ways information can be displayed.

With a little help and guidance about reading nonfiction, you can feel good about introducing a young reader to the world of *EZ Readers* nonfiction books.

Mitchell Lane
PUBLISHERS

2001 SW 31st Avenue
Hallandale, FL 33009
www.mitchelllane.com

First Edition, 2020.

Author: Robert Scally
Designer: Ed Morgan
Editor: Sharon F. Doorasamy

Names/credits:
Title: All About African Lions / by Robert Scally
Description: Hallandale, FL : Mitchell Lane Publishers, [2020]

Series: Animals Around the World
Library bound ISBN: 9781680203936
eBook ISBN: 9781680203943

EZ readers is an imprint of Mitchell Lane Publishers

Library of Congress Cataloging-in-Publication Data
Names: Scally, Robert, 1958- author.
Title: All about the African lion / by Robert Scally.
Description: First edition. | Hallandale, FL : EZ Readers, an imprint of Mitchell Lane Publishers, 2020. | Series: Animals around the world-Africa animals | Includes bibliographical references and index.
Identifiers: LCCN 2018028570| ISBN 9781680203936 (library bound) | ISBN 9781680203943 (ebook)
Subjects: LCSH: Lion—Africa—Juvenile literature.
Classification: LCC QL737.C23 S2856 2020 | DDC 599.75/5—dc23
LC record available at https://lccn.loc.gov/2018028570

Photo credits: Freepik.com, cover photo: Alexas_Fotos Pixabay, p. 4-5 Michael Steinberg Unsplash, p. 6-7 Klinkow Pixabay, p. 8-9 Alexas_Fotos Pixabay, p. 10-11 Jean Wimmerlan Unsplash, p. 12-13 Thomas Retterath Shutterstock, p. 14-15 AjayLalu Pixabay, p. 16-17 Srivari Unsplash, p. 18-19 Wolfgang Franz Shutterstock, p. 20-21 Shireah Ragnar on Unsplash, mapchart.net

CONTENTS

African lions are cats. Lions are like house cats in some ways. Both have claws. Both have paws.

Lions are different from other cats. Only male lions have a **mane**. The mane is the fur around a male lion's face.

A female lion is called a **lioness**. Female lions do not have manes.

Lions are the only cats with fur at the end of their tails. The fur is called a **tuft**.

A lion family is called a **pride**.
A baby lion is called a **cub**.

Lions roar loudly. Lions roar louder than all other big cats. A lion's roar is as loud as a car horn honking right next to you.

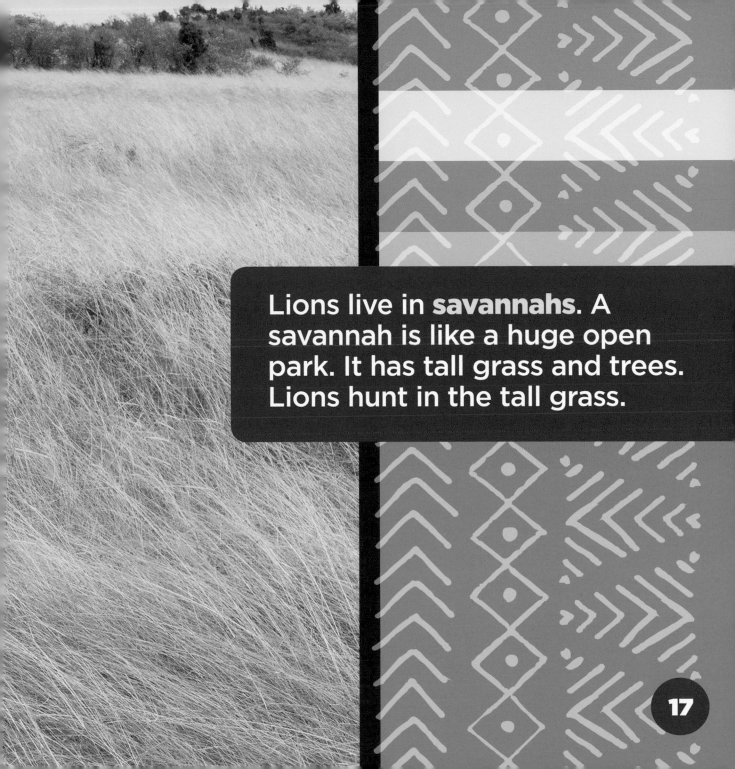

Lions live in **savannahs**. A savannah is like a huge open park. It has tall grass and trees. Lions hunt in the tall grass.

Lions are hunters. They eat meat. Animals that lions eat are zebras, warthogs, giraffes, and **impalas**.

Lions sleep most of the day. They hunt at night.

21

WHERE DO LIONS LIVE?

Tanzania
Kenya
South Africa
Botswana
Zambia
Zimbabwe

INTERESTING FACTS

- Lions live 10 to 18 years in the wild.

- A lion's roar can be heard up to five miles away.

- Female lions do the hunting.

- Female and male lions look different. Males and females of other kinds of cats look the same.

- Lions can sleep 20 hours a day.

- Lions have five toes on their front paws with four toes on their back paws.

- Lions can see six times better in the dark than people.

PARTS OF A LION

Mane
Only male lions have manes. They are the only cats with manes.

Paws
Lions have toes with fur around them. The fur helps lions walk quietly.

Claws
Lions use their claws for fighting and climbing.

Teeth
Lions have sharp teeth. Lions use their teeth for killing other animals.

Tail
Lions have fur on the end of their tails called a tuft.

GLOSSARY

cub
A baby lion

impala
An antelope

lioness
A female lion

mane
The fur around a male lion's face

pride
A group of lions

savannah
A part of Africa with grass and trees

tuft
Fur on the end of a lion's tail

FURTHER READING

Felix, Ina. *Lions: Children Book of Fun Facts & Amazing Photos on Animals in Nature*. CreateSpace Independent Publishing Platform, 2016.

Marsh, Laura. *National Geographic Readers: Lions*. Washington, DC: National Geographic Kids, 2015.

Joubert, Beverly, and Joubert, Dereck. *Face to Face with Lions (Face to Face with Animals)*. Washington, DC: National Geographic, 2010.

ON THE INTERNET

Basic Facts About Lions
https://defenders.org/lion/basic-facts

African Lions—All the Fascinating Facts You Were Looking For
https://www.africa-wildlife-detective.com/african-lions.html

How Many Teeth Does a Lion Have?
https://www.reference.com/pets-animals/many-teeth-lion-9c0130aa8177b5f3#

INDEX